To E.

Peter

On Life

A Collection of
Poems and Writings

With love

Anita

December
2021

xx   xc

By
PETER DANBY

THE CHOIR PRESS

First published in the United Kingdom in 2021 by

The Choir Press

ISBN 978-1-78963-226-2

Extracts from the poem *Aftermath* copyright Siegfried Sassoon with permission kindly granted by the Estate of George Sassoon

Contents

The Beginning

I always liked the idea of publishing a book. Partly to win and enjoy worldwide acclaim, of course, and partly to leave something of my life experience and lessons learnt for others. Yet, every time a theme emerged and I could see the idea taking shape, I would find the book, already written, in some bookstore or library.

This, then is my solution. There are other books of poems, but these are my own and the stories about their origins are all mine. They capture something of those life experiences and the lessons I have taken from them. I have found the writing of poetry quite therapeutic at times of heightened emotion – or perhaps, deep troughs might be a better description in some cases. I have attempted to set the scene and explain the background to some but not all the poems – some are just random writings. I hope you enjoy them.

I don't remember being particularly drawn to poetry as a young boy or at school. In particular, I enjoyed the war poets, Wilfred Owen and Siegfried Sassoon, but I wrote nothing of my own. Nor can I remember what prompted me to write the following verses when I was at university. We sang the songs of Max Boyce, the Welsh bard, in our rugby club and maybe it was an attempt to emulate him.

This first poem reflects something of me at that time of my life. Just to set the scene, Dai was a prop forward in the days when rugby prop forwards were expected to be big, strong and not do much more than wrestle with the opposition prop forwards in the scrum. Any handling or running skills were a bonus. Dave Spiller and Dave Porter were his front row colleagues. Barry John, like Dai was a Welsh rugby player; perhaps one of the greatest. He represented Wales and the British Lions but more even than that, he brought a magical quality to the game; his dexterity, his wonderful tactical awareness and the shimmering brilliance of his running and ability to ghost past defenders.

It was a light-hearted poem designed to gently laugh at ourselves and to celebrate the characters, both the famous internationals and those from our own happy band, that brought joy to our lives. I always felt it 'read' better in a real or imaginary Welsh accent.

Dai Jones, The Great

As we took the field against Portsmouth Poly,
Dai had no dreams of any glory.
He shirked the limelight and the fame,
He only played 'cos he loved the game.

But then, by some sudden quirk of fate,
Dai became 'Dai Jones, the Great';
As 'neath that grey and cloudy sky,
He scored a truly magic try.

On the 25, he took the ball,
'Go for the line' went up the call;
And the Poly winger tried in vain,
To catch Dai's golden, flowing mane.

With Porter's grin and Spiller's hug,
Dai took it all with a modest shrug.
But, when Judgement Day has come and gone,
They will seat him next to Barry John.

Warrior Days Ending

The Army was never meant to be a career. I joined up in 1979 on a 3-year, short service commission to experience some challenge and adventure before resuming a career somewhere in the business world. Three years became four and then more as I joined the Commando Forces and continued to enjoy the life. Then, I passed an exam and qualified to go the Army Staff College. To go, I had to take a regular commission and commit to a minimum of 16 years.

I was happy to do so. I was highly regarded and moving up the ladder, I was now married with two young children and the army provided a secure, respected and – very important – enjoyable life.

Then, in my first staff (office) job, I encountered a very different type of work and a very autocratic general. They sparked a questioning within me; 'what kind of work do I want to do and what kind of person do I want to be'. You might imagine, there was a great deal of heart searching and fear – I was contemplating giving up a great deal and taking a risk not just for my own future but my family too.

One of the fundamentals that I kept coming back to was my desire for freedom, for autonomy. While I had a wonderful freedom in my early days in the army, I could feel the constraints of the military world beginning to close around me and see the path ahead beginning to narrow. But to leave? There would be no security, no safety net – I had nothing more than an idea of what I might do and no pension or income to fall back on. I wrote this poem to give myself the strength to take the step. I saw the first two lines on a picture in a rock-climbing magazine – the rest came from my own restless heart.

Take the Step

To be all you can be you must dream to be more.

To achieve all that is possible, you must attempt the impossible.

So, look to the skies, step off the ledge and fly free.

Where the only limits are those you set yourself;

Where you may soar as high as you dare, and then go higher.

Take courage, be true to yourself, take the step ...

And why the picture of a seagull? Just after I left the army, I met with a business woman called Jenny Bailey to get some advice on this new world I was entering. She gave me a beautiful book of inspirational writings produced by the people who worked in her company. It included some quotes from Richard Bach's book, Jonathon Livingston Seagull. It is a magical story and Jonathon has remained an inspiration to me. Have a read of the book.

The Journey of Discovery

While I was preparing to leave the army and begin a new career, I attended a workshop called Personal Power, run by an inspiring character called Mark Layder. He encouraged me to begin to explore different aspects of myself. Soon after leaving the army, that exploration continued when I attended a facilitation programme at University of Surrey which further challenged me to open myself to feelings, emotions – of myself and others. It was an unsettling experience for a young man priding himself on his physical toughness. Soon after one of the Surrey modules I found myself walking the streets in Prague reflecting deeply on life, my life and the changes it brings.

An old man approached me, a beggar. Bearded, straggly hair, dirty hands and face, walking with a stoop and dressed in an old coat, I can see his face now; his eyes, as I looked into them and his hand open towards me begging for a few coins. I put my hand in my pocket and felt for some coins. There weren't any, only notes. So, what could I do? Something in his eyes held me. I placed a note in his hand, smiled and closed my hands around his. He looked down, saw the note and tears sprang into his eyes – and into mine as my heart was pierced by his look of gratitude. It was an experience, a feeling I will never forget and the gift that old man gave me on that day was worth far more than the piece of paper I placed in his hand. When I returned to my hotel, I tried to capture something of what this all meant to me.

A Knight's Tale

Now, safe in the fortress of my mind
And bold with the sword of my thinking,
I take up the shield of my ancestors
And set out on the hero's quest.

Oh, how strong, how good I feel.
Matching each foe blow for blow.
With speed and guile ever quickening,
I am that hero, perhaps even a God.

But gentle lady, what sweet agony is this?
How can it be, a hero fallen thus?
No blade, nor arrow could cut so deep,
Strike so fast yet leave no mark.

Oh, darkest night! Oh, cold despair!
My armour lies broken around me,
The sword heavy in my hand,
As your pain touches and tears my heart.

Oh, wondrous light. Oh, gentle beauty,
Calling my soul to wake.
What love pours from that opened heart;
What power from your mighty Will?

Now, safe within these loving arms;
And bold with the sword of Truth,
I lay down the shield of my old king
And set out on the holy quest.

Searching for Meaning

After leaving the army in 1992, I trained as a healer and began to study in a mystical school – reconnecting with and exploring the strong spiritual impulse I had first experienced as a young child. I like to think it opened dimensions of my being that had lain dormant as I enjoyed life as a young warrior. It has led me to write my own philosophy of life, drawing on sacred writings and teachings from around the world. And, of course, it is my own answer to that impossible question, 'why?'

Travelling the world, seeing the incredible technological advances and the privileged lives of the wealthy (and I include myself in that group). Travelling the world, seeing the depths of poverty, of violence and abuse. How often do I ask the question, 'why'? Is there any meaning or purpose to what seems to be the lottery of life? My own understanding, drawn from my mystical studies and my own life experiences is that 'yes, there is'. I should perhaps explain the opening words of the poem are from the Vedic traditions; Atman, the seed of light or, what we might call the soul of each person and Brahman, the universal 'force' the source of all that is and all that will be. What some might call, God.

Why?

Atman in Brahman, Brahman in Atman;
We are all a part of the whole
And we live each life in its service
And to further develop our soul.

That soul has lived many lives
And every life that we chose,
Was linked to both those great missions;
As, from the darkness we rose.

So, you see, the suffering of others
And the lives that are filled full of pain,
Are not without meaning or purpose;
Each life is lived for our gain.

The lessons, if we can just see them,
Are lessons of anger and hate;
But also, of love and compassion
And the patience to struggle or wait.

So, the beggar who lies in the doorway
Or the refugees on the beach,
Might just be great souls, who have chosen
To come back in this life, to teach.

So, look once again at your life;
And see it and the world in this light.
As a world that is meant for our learning
And not just a hell where we fight.

And as, through our lives, we awaken
And feel our consciousness shift,
The veils of darkness will open
And we will see every life as a gift.

So, yes, each life has a purpose;
We are all a part of the whole.
And, each life is lived in its service
And to further develop the soul.

Choosing Our Path

Back in 2007, I began to do some volunteer work in Thailand. That was the beginning of a journey that has led to the creation of a charity, called Small Acts of Kindness. One of the projects has been working with young girls in Nepal. One of the girls on the first programme I ran there was given away for 'adoption' (in Nepal, that usually means some form of domestic service) when she was two years old. She showed me a poem, which she wrote to her mother; a poem of her deep gratitude and love. As I was brushing the tears from my cheeks, she explained. Her mother knew that the only chance her daughter had of a better life than her own, away from the sexual and physical abuse, was to give her away. Imagine the sacrifice, the pain of giving away your two-year old little girl. Imagine the world those girls and women live in. In so many countries, they live their lives in servitude, in fear. In Nigeria, a colleague of mine asked a father, living in the north of the country the reason that his 10-year old daughter had never been outside of their home – not once, not for school, not to play. His answer, 'What for'?

I have seen all of that. I have heard the arguments. 'Peter, you do not understand. It is our culture'. I cannot find any part of myself that does not find it abhorrent. I cannot find any part of myself which does not cry out for, work for, fight for such abuse and such injustice to end.

So, why then, do I feel so challenged by the feminist movement in my own culture, in my own country. Is it just the fear of loss as the balance of power shifts? I see women encouraged to take on what the Chinese would describe as Yang characteristics, male qualities – be strong, be forceful and dominant and I feel my male instinct prodding me to respond with an even stronger force? I see the Divine Feminine no longer invoked to bring love, compassion and balance but used to champion the fight to overpower the patriarchy. Do we really, need more violence, physical or mental, in our world?

Feminism is just one cause. There are now so many labels, so many divisions in our society and while I laud the fight for fairness and justice, I see how quickly now each group – whatever gender, race, faith or other description – judges, condemns and attacks those who do not share their beliefs.

One of the reasons I take my charity work to other countries is my own belief that we need to work across boundaries, between communities and between countries, if we are to change the endless pattern of hatred and violence. We must work to bring people together and seek to overcome the divisions which stem from our animal, instinctive nature rather than blame, shame and attack.

This is the background to two poems I wrote beside the sea in Winchelsea and another, later poem. My own quest for harmony in a divided world. The first, is Seek the Light and the second is Light and Shadow – the Challenge of Life. The later poem is called The Endless Fight and reflects my quest to find some way out of the endless cycle of conflict between race, religions, gender and so many other divides in our world.

Seek the Light

It used to be just boys,
Were taught to stand and fight.
To show how strong and brave we are,
To stand for what is right.

But now at every turn,
Each young girl is told,
To let their voice ring out;
Be strong, be brave, be bold.

And what of care and kindness,
Of nurturing and love;
As all now strive for power
To be the one above.

As long as power blinds us,
To who and what we are,
The world will soon be rid of us;
Another empty star.

Within each man and woman,
In every girl and boy,
There is a quiet soul
Of light and love and joy.

That soul is an expression,
Of a timeless seed of light.
A part of something greater;
Beyond touch, sound or sight.

We see ourselves divided,
By class or sex or skin.
We do not see the light
That radiates within.

It's a never- ending journey;
As that soul keeps moving on.
From one life to another;
Now a daughter, now a son.

And the aim of life is not to win
More money or more power.
It is to let that seed of light,
Take root, grow tall and flower.

So, next time you are angered
And feel the need to fight,
Reach down into your soul;
To the kindness, love and light.

See beyond the differences
Of age, of sex, of skin;
And seek the beauty of the light
That radiates within.

Light and Shadow

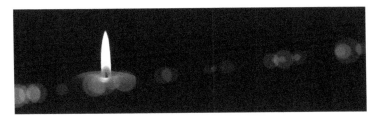

In my own country, in many parts of the Western world, we have become more and more aware of the inequalities in life. On the positive side, it has led to a championing of supressed groups and a policing of abusive or offensive behaviours. On the negative side, each activist group, every group fighting for their own cause seems to be driving us further from a world of peace and harmony. Rather than acceptance, each group seeks to force their own judgements and beliefs on others, ignoring the warning of Friedrich Nietzsche

> "Beware that, when fighting monsters, you yourself do not become a monster ... for when you gaze long into the abyss. The abyss gazes also into you."

It's easy to judge others, easy to see the good in our own tribe or group and to denigrate, demean others. Our survival as a species has always depended on building a strong sense of self and a strong group around us. The expression 'birds of a feather, flock together' is born from our instinctive drive to move towards those who share common traits. We may not be able to change our instinctive drives, but we need to be aware of them if we are to make choices that will lead to that more equitable world.

Light and Shadow – the Challenge of Life

We like to think we're special,
Better than the rest.
It's written in our nature,
To see ourselves as best.

We laugh or sneer at others
To prove that we are right.
And then, if we are challenged,
Quick to clash or fight.

Colour, gender, tribe,
How we speak or dress
Will spark that instinct in us
And relax or cause us stress.

It's not that we are racist,
Or cruel in our ways;
It's just the animal inside,
That strives to keep us safe.

The challenge that we face,
As always it has been,
Is to be aware and understand
Those drives that lie unseen.

To know that animal inside
And recognise its voice;
But listen to our Higher Self,
Before we make our choice.

To act and speak with love,
Not anger, greed and spite;
To seek to understand,
Not act with hate and fight.

So, yes, each one is special,
Or holds the power to be;
But we also have a shadow
That is easy not to see.

To be a force for good,
And choose what we know is right,
We must recognise that shadow
And move towards the light.

Breaking the Chains

In the last couple of years, the Black Lives Matter movement has impacted on my views of race. I was invited to join a multi-racial group to explore racism through reading and conversation. I was also invited to co-facilitate a session in a University of Oxford college exploring how we can move towards an anti-racist culture. I wrote the following script to read to the group before entering a dialogue; not a conversation or debate, with each party fighting for their corner, but a dialogue where we explore and seek understanding together.

I watch the white policeman brutally assault the black man in our modern streets and the films of his ancestors ripped from their homes and crammed into ships to cross the Atlantic. I watch the young Yemeni child lying, limbless in his mother's arms – or is it a Syrian child. I watch the old films of the walking skeletons emerging from Auschwitz and Belsen and the new ones of rockets, fired into the streets of Gaza. I see the rows of Tutsi skulls in Rwanda, slaughtered by their neighbours. I see the young girl, shivering as she waits to be thrown to the next man who pays her master so he can rape her and the young boy, his face melted by the acid his mother poured over him to help her begging.

Everywhere I look, I can point the finger at injustice, at the vileness of a people, a race, including my own. I see darkness in every human heart, man and woman, when the light is blocked. We need to find a way to let the light that is within us, shine out. We can fight endlessly, I know that. You attack me and claim to be the victim. I deny your story, retaliate and claim I am the victim. You deny my accusation, attack me again and claim to be the real victim. On and on, we go. A cycle that will only be broken by riot, imprisonment, a machete or a bullet. We can point an accusing finger at others and talk of our own greatness or our own suffering – we have done so for thousands of years. Or we can seek a new way. It is time to break the chains that bind us. It is time to open the doors in our own mind and to open the doors that keep us apart.

How do I prepare myself – heart and mind – for a dialogue. To enter a conversation with an open mind rather than clouded with my life stories and all the prejudices that arise from them. Here is a ritual that I have created.

Begin by settling into a mindful state – sit comfortably, relax the mind and bring your attention into your physical body, right here right now. Deepen your breath and gently close your eyes. Listen to my voice, imagine it as your voice and just notice how the words touch you.

Beginning a Conversation

Wait, my friend, do not speak for a moment. Before I can see you clearly, before I can hear your story, I must quieten the beast that lives within me and watches to keep me safe. I must clear the clouds from my eyes and still the voices in my mind.

You need to know who I am. You need to know that the beast is a part of me, yet with a mind of its own, and that it is strong. You need to know those voices – the critic, the clown, the cynic, the child - they never leave me however much I wish they would. You need to understand that those clouds are the stories of my past, and they colour all that I see and hear. The beast heard those stories too and is quick to see a threat. You need to know that, though I shout out for justice and the rights of all, I can be a racist too.

Know this. I have already judged you, shamed though I feel to do so. I see the colour of your skin, I hear the sound of your voice and you are cast, already in my stories; hero or villain, friend or foe. I see your shape, your gender and the cut of your clothes. I see you how you stand or walk and how you look at me. And already, I know who you are and what you stand for – in my stories.

Know this. When you shout at me and call me names, I cannot stop the beast from waking and opening his claws. When your voice goes on and on, condemning me or my tribe, then those voices in my mind grow ever louder – shouting to drown out your words, challenge your story.

Know this. I am that beast, but I am, too, a kind loving soul. I am a racist, but I am, too, a pure seed of light. I am a killer and a saint. I am a thief and a generous, giving heart. I am a selfish, greedy man and I am a part of all that is. I am one with all life. Let me quieten the beast that lives within me, clear the clouds from my own eyes and still those voices in my mind. Now, I can hear your story and I can laugh and weep with you.

Wait, my friend, do not speak for a moment. Before you tell me your story, you must first quieten the beast that lives within you, clear the clouds from your eyes and still the voices in your mind.

I know that you have already judged me and you are right to do so. But did you see all of me? Did you see the racist, misogynistic old man or did you see the love that sits in my heart? Who would you speak with, whom will you tell your story to? Do you wish to wound and hurt, to have your revenge – I know that my own beast would and is expecting that from you? Or do you wish to touch my soul and for us to walk and work together in this precious life?

So, now, tell me your story. Let me sit beside you and be with you, not the enemy to attack. Speak softly so that our beasts – yours and mine – stay quiet and the voice of our souls can be heard.

And I will tell you my story too, it is a part of this, it is a part of our story. Let us, for a moment in time, sit side by side and see each other as we really, are – not the shadow that we fear, although we are aware of that - but the light that shines within us both, within us all, the light that makes us one.

The Nature of Change

In my leadership development, I have attended many workshops to develop my own skills and gain more knowledge. I wrote this on an MBTI workshop. MBTI is a psychometric instrument to help assess different dimensions of our personality. We were given the task of describing change and then split into small groups according to our personal preferences in these different dimensions. As the only introvert in the group, I was more than happy to sit in a corner on my own and write …

Change is natural. As above, so below. As without, so within. We grow older every day and so do our children.

Resistance to change brings stagnation in both mind and body and it is the same in an organisation. Change is life affirming. It is life.

But it is also death. It involves all that death means to us; the fear, the loss, the grieving.

It means letting go of something that we have grown to love – a person, a thing or an old habit.

Yet, in the letting go – if we really, let go – then we move into a new birth, a new experience, a freshness and vitality. A new life.

To fully embrace change is to fully embrace both life and death. It is the circle of life.

To fully embrace change is to acknowledge and let go of fear, to become fully alive.

It is to learn to hold a loved one, and ourselves, lightly. It is to see the wonder in each passing moment, in each breath.

The extroverts, the logical thinkers and practical types were surprised that all this could come from sitting alone in a corner and amused that it contained no list or no action points. But it also touched one or two deeply.

Our Beautiful World

Ifind it easy in our modern world to feel a sense of darkness around us. The media bring us the news of war and atrocities but also focus our attention on every failing, every misspoken word. Social media encourages us to judge, compare and, all too quickly, condemn. So, in many of my poems, my poetry is a way for me to make sense of that feeling. In this poem, I was looking to bring my attention to the beauty and wonder of the world we are a part of.

Did you ever sit beside the sea,
To watch the setting sun
And feel a sense of wonder;
With nature feel as one?

Did you stand beside a mountain
Beneath the peaks so high;
And feel a sense of awe
As you gaze towards the sky?

Did you ever see an eagle
Soaring in that sky;
And feel a sense of joy,
As your spirit leapt to fly?

Did you ever hold a new born babe
Close against your chest,
And feel that surge of joy,
Fill your heart and breast?

Did you see an act of kindness,
Somewhere, in some place
And feel a smile rise within you
And beam across your face?

Did you feel the rush of pleasure
When you scored or won the game?
Did you feel that same elation
When your children did the same?

All that we are told of,
Is a world of bile and hate;
And it's sometimes hard to remember
How much is good and great.

That for every act of darkness,
There is a beam of light.
For every act of greed and hate,
There are those who do what's right.

And each of us holds the balance.
We can choose to act with greed,
Or seek to walk a higher path
And give what others need.

We can all act through instinct;
The way of fight and flight.
Or, choose to walk a higher path
Of kindness, love and light.

So, go and stand beside the sea,
Or 'neath the moon at night.
Feel the power grow within
And let the light shine bright

Be Here, Now

I have drawn much from the Buddha's teachings and they have greatly influenced my own philosophy and understanding of life and the nature of things. My very limited understanding of quantum physics is that our modern scientists would support the idea that all things, at the sub-atomic level, are constantly moving into and out of existence, constantly changing.

I wrote this next poem in an attempt to make sense of that; to unite the idea of eternal life that I learnt in my childhood religious education and the transient nature of our own bodies, of the world we live in.

Nothing is as it seems.
Can you catch a ray of dancing sunlight at the breaking of the day? And hold it. No, It has gone. And yet, it is here, now.

Can you see in the eyes of a newborn child your own purity and love? And hold them. No, they have gone. And yet, they are here now.

Can you hold the hand of a loved one, tightly to you? And let it go. They have gone. And yet, they are here, now.

Can you feel the tender touch of a loving soul in your own heart? And hold it. It has already gone. And yet you can feel it, now.

Nothing is as it seems; we cannot hold the passing moment. It has gone. And yet nothing is lost. No word, no thought, no feeling. It lives within us. It is here, now.

We are everything we have ever been and everything we will ever be. What has gone forever is in us now, forever.

Nothing is as it seems. Nothing stays the same. The joy of today is tomorrow's pain; the burnt-out ashes of our dreams and fantasies leaves space for new growth.

So, can we sit with our own joy and our own pain without guilt or shame?

Can we laugh gently at our own pride and vanity and fear? Can we take them into our heart – and let them go?

Can we hold tight to our own centre, to our own sense of being? And let even that go.

The last breath merges with the first. The seed of life and light grows from the darkness. The sun rises and sets.

We are here, now. That is all.

Discovery Learning
in Israel

In February, 2018, I visited Israel as part of a business school programme. The participants were encouraged to draw lessons and insights from the whole range of experiences they were given and the thoughts and feelings that arose as a result of those experiences; a process we call Discovery Learning. We visited the temple, the wailing wall and walked the streets of Jerusalem. We saw a blooded young Palestinian being dragged away by the security forces and, later, listened to a debate between Israeli and Palestinian speakers. We visited start-ups in vibrant Tel Aviv, a refugee centre and admired the street art on the building walls. We saw the sun rise over the Negev desert and soaked in the atmosphere of this beautiful land. I was moved by the reflections that the participants wrote – deep insights on their own lives as well as the country they had visited. So, I decided to write my own. Here it is.

The Holy Land

Ah, Israel! What beauty lies here; what spirits have fed this land. A land to touch the soul; a treasure for the world.

Yet, how life, how light and darkness both nourish but also cut and savage your beauty. How deeply scarred now are your beautiful body, mind and spirit?

Here is heaven and hell set together in the cradle of our world. The warm sands set alongside towering rocks and shards. The ancient desert lands stained with the blood of neighbours, of sisters and brothers. The vibrant pathways of history, of silk and spice, flowing through this blessed land now blocked with wire and walls, stemming the flow of peoples, of poetry, of peace.

A new nation growing from the seeds that survived the killing fires. A fresh impulse of inspiration and hope to quicken the pulse, cut new paths and new ways. Such vibrant work, so many wondrous notes of compassion and kindness sounded in a land held tight within by the binding, unforgiving words of religion, surrounded without, by hostility and hate.

Victims for three thousand years or more, how your pain has toughened and hardened you. Fighters in a harsh land and a harsher world; now using the qualities of your own survival to build a dynamic, new world even as you stifle the freedom of those who share this land.

Ah, Israel! A mirror of the pathways to my own soul. A heart of gold, torn and slashed with the devils of my needs and fears. A spirit aching to soar free, bound tight by the limits of the beliefs and judgements that each hold to be the only truth. Good intentions broken on the rocks of my hubris; the special one, the chosen one.

So, thank you for the reminders; for that mirror you hold for me and my own country. Even as I sit here in judgement, I begin to see more clearly both the greatness and the great injustice and unfairness on my own doorstep, the tensions between 'tribes' simmering beneath the surface of politeness. I begin to see my own judgements reflected as my own intolerance and prejudice.

So, thank you for the reminder, 'to forgive those who trespass against us' before the grudges fester into open, bleeding wounds. A reminder to let the energy flow between us before ignorance turns to suspicion and then hatred. A reminder to step back far enough from my own view of the mountain that I might see what others see – and that it is also 'the truth'. To hold to my own values, but not so tightly that others might not breathe freely too. To fight for what is right but to be careful that I do not begin to mirror and become that which I fight against.

Thank you, Israel, for showing me who I am, the light and darkness. I hope that you may find a path to walk in peace and that we may all do the same.

Seeking a Higher Path

In 2012, the Mayan calendar finished a 'great cycle' and there were predictions of the end of the world. It feels now, as though those predictions are coming to pass – just maybe a bit later. With all that is going on in the world – the climate, the refugees, the wars, the human trafficking, the extinction of so many species, the pollution of the rivers and oceans – it is hard to stay positive and optimistic for our own species. Indeed, it feels as though it would be a blessing for life on Earth if we were removed from it. For all our self-proclaimed intelligence and 'progress', our modern world is driven by the same animal instincts which enabled us to survive and thrive in the primitive past.

This poem is my attempt to draw on the teachings I have experienced over the years to give meaning to this world of light and dark, dark shadow. It is even more relevant now as we endure the Covid 19 pandemic.

A Higher Path

They say that with every child,
The world begins anew;
And the lessons, so hard learnt,
Are lost, like morning dew.

The wisdom of a lifetime,
Gathered over years;
From happiness and sorrow,
Laughter, love and tears.

And if not lost, then buried
In books that gather dust.
Unheard in words grown soft with age,
In a world of cut and thrust.

Yet, though these words lie hidden,
That's how it's meant to be.
For the aim of life is learning;
To discover how to be.

It's not the wealth or power,
That show how much we've grown;
It's who we have become,
The seeds that we have sown.

And here's the irony of life,
As we search for harmony;
It's through that endless conflict,
That we grow from seed to tree.

If we can tame our instinct
And let the soul fly free,
Then we will find that hidden gold
And be, all that we can be.

And then, for just an instant,
We may live with peace and love;
As we see beyond the turmoil,
To a higher path above.

And, then the cycle turns again,
Our ashes turn to dust;
And a new-born babe cries out for love
In a word of fear and lust.

But as our spirit leaves this world
And travels on its way,
An essence of our soul is left,
Embedded in this clay.

And as our light grows brighter
As each life's work is done,
We move closer to that greater light
From which we all have come.

The Voice of Silence
(or The Introvert's Lament)

I was in the Western desert in Egypt waiting for the sunset. It is a special moment – the beauty always touches something deep within me. Also at the viewing point was a group of tourists who were talking and laughing in loud voices. They seemed to be unaware of the changing colours of the sky, and the sounds of the desert were drowned by their noise. I felt angry that they were taking this moment away from me and a sense of sadness that they would miss the wonder of this moment in time. I wondered, 'why do people find it so hard to sit in silence'?

I was standing with a group of friends who were chatting to a local of the country. Content and reflecting deeply on a leadership programme I had been working on, I was asked by this complete stranger, 'Why do you say nothing? Why are you silent'?

In that reflective state, this question that has been asked of me by many people over the years prompted these thoughts. I hope that they may help you understand …

'Why do you say nothing? Why are you silent'? Well, listen for a moment to my silence and perhaps you will hear.

In my silence, I can hear the voices of my own mind not that of others.

I can hear a voice that brings clarity to my thoughts and helps me pick more carefully the words with which I can express them – or decide not to.

I can hear a voice that helps my ideas take root and grow or sends them swirling away into endless space.

In my silence, I can hear the voice of my body and the energy that moves and feeds it.

A voice that lets my emotions run free within the walls of this temple; to rage, to weep, to laugh or shout with joy without fear or concern for how they might be seen or heard by others.

A voice that tells me I am alive and of all that lives and breathes around me.

A voice that tells me something about you too, my friend, about your nature and how I should be with you.

And in my silence, I can hear the voice of my soul. The quiet voice that can light the fires or calm the storm.

The voice of the ancients, of wisdom; of truth expressed with love.

So, can you hear? In my silence, I am not silent at all – if you can also just stop for a moment and listen.

But thank you, for asking; I need your voice too. Your words and questions stir the voices within me. And perhaps you can you hear all of that too, if you are silent for a moment. So, still that voice that you hear most often and let me stir within you, the voice of silence.

The War to End All Wars

I had just returned from Rwanda. I stayed in Nyamata and visited a large church which is now a genocide memorial. 10,000 Tutsi men, women and children came to this place of refuge only to be slaughtered inside the walls. 50,000 lie buried in the grounds. On the last day, in Kigali, I walked around the genocide memorial with my friend, Jean d'Amour. Over 250,000 are buried there. Jean was just 7 years old when he lost his entire family in the killings and I could not bring myself to look at his face as we read, heard and saw the stories of the survivors.

Each year, my village cricket team play a memorial game with the Siegfried Sassoon Fellowship. A son of the village, Siegfried was one of the great war poets and, after winning a Military Cross, he spoke out strongly against the conduct of the war. Each year I read one of his poems at the end of the game, it's called The Aftermath and contains a heart wrenching message. Below are some of the words from his poem.

Have you forgotten yet? ... For the world's events have rumbled on since those gagged days ... Look down and swear by the slain of the War that you'll never forget ... Do you remember the rats; and the stench..of corpses rotting in front of the front-line trench- ... And dawn coming, dirty-white, and chill with a hopeless rain? ... Do you ever stop and ask, 'Is it all going to happen again? 'Have you forgotten yet? ... Look up, and swear by the green of the spring that you'll never forget.

And then, as we remembered the Battle of The Somme, where some 800,000 died in the beautiful French countryside I was reading reports from around the world – Syria, Yemen, Afghanistan, Libya – and could feel my spirit sinking further into a dark abyss. And, finally, in my own country, my England, it was the time of the Brexit referendum; the beginning of one of the most divisive periods in our history, shattering the bonds which have held us together as a nation.

I was in a dark place and wrote this, as a way of helping myself find a path out of that darkness.

One Hundred Years since
The Battle of The Somme
The War to End All Wars

'The war to end all wars',
That is what they said.
How sad those words seem now,
How many more are dead?

Each year we all remember;
Their names we still revere.
Each year we keep on killing;
No end to hate and fear.

So why does nothing change?
What makes us fight and slay?
Can we ever find an answer?
Or do we just hope and pray?

We wish for some new prophet
Or a champion of right;
But we seem to be unable
To live in peace, not fight.

The answer's very simple,
If only we can see;
It is not to blame each other,
For the problem lies with me.

It is always 'them', not 'us',
It is always 'them' not 'me';
But in all, sit good and evil,
We must each, choose how to be.

There is no end to hatred,
For always some will choose
To kill, to rape and plunder;
Use power to abuse.

Always slaves and masters,
Those who grasp for fame
Or fortune or more power;
It's a never-ending game.

Unless we learn to master
The animal inside;
To act with good intention
And not let instinct guide.

There is within each person,
In every girl and boy,
A loving soul and spirit
With light and love and joy

And we must help those children
Awake that hidden light;
And seek to live in peace,
Not judge, and hate and fight.

And the only way to help.
Is the very hardest way.
It means that I and you
Must 'do' and not just 'say'.

So, next time you are crossed,
Are angry, feeling hate;
Before you speak or act,
Stop, breathe deep and wait.

Remember where it leads us,
That animal inside,
The endless fields of poppies
And the guilt and shame we hide.

It's not in wars and battles,
That we face our greatest fight.
It's in the daily struggle,
To do what we know is right.

And in that endless struggle,
It's easy to give in,
As others all around us
Laugh and play to 'win'.

But there's more to life than winning
Or having more and more.
The soul takes nothing with it
When we reach that final door.

The only thing that matters,
When all is said and done,
Is the essence of your soul,
Of what you have become.

The war to end all wars
Was not some distant fight.
It's here and now, in you and I,
Each morning, noon and night.

So, stop, breathe deep and wait.
Let fear and hatred rest.
Let's you and I, together
Face this eternal test.

At around the same time and for the same purpose I wrote

The Choice

Will it ever end:
The lies, the treachery, the selfish greed and lust for
power?
Will it ever end;
The abuse, the endless quest for more, for bigger, for
better than you?

No, my friend, it will never end.
Always the race begins again as soon as the killing ceases
Vengeance calls before the blood has soaked away.
The young prepare for battle as the already old, weep.

So why even start,
When we know our dreams must fade?
Why start afresh, why bother at all,
When the sands we build on are shifting still?

Why? Because that is who we are. That is life.
The acorn sprouts as the old oak dies.
Ashes to ashes as the new babe cries.
Love and hate; the endless cycle of life.

Within each of us sits light and darkness.
We all know anger, we all feel joy.
We can all hate and we can all forgive
It is for us to choose.

As some will build, so some destroy
There is no right without wrong.
There is no love without hate
It is for us to choose.

So, we try do what is right,
Not what others do.
We try to live with love, not hate
We try to forgive and judge only our self.

Hold back the need to wound or kill.
Hold back the words that cut and hurt.
Pick up the pieces and begin again.
Heal the wounds and rebuild afresh.

No, it will never end
The great circle of life; light and darkness need each other.
Just choose the light. Be the light.
It is the right thing to do, nothing more. Make the right
choice.

The Stream of Life

In the Israeli Museum in Jerusalem, there is a quotation on the wall of one of the displays'

'Biology enables, Culture forbids'

My experience in the museum, in visiting the many historic sites and witnessing the impact of culture on this land led me to build on that quotation and write the following:

> Nature enables, culture forbids. Nature adapts, culture restricts. Nature is governed by unbending, universal principles, culture by social rules and subjective judgement. Nature is the Truth. Culture is a set of beliefs that seek to define the Truth. Nature is an endless stream, culture is a moment in time.

The closer we are to nature, the closer we are to the infinite, to the endless cycle of birth, death and rebirth. Closer to the forces of creation and destruction, to the forming, reforming and disintegration of all things.

We cannot capture the essence of life in a book. It is beyond words, beyond formulae and definitions which, immediately draw boundaries and restrict. Life, the spirit is boundless.

And always, we are in the flow. The stream of life; the great orbits of the stars, the ocean currents, the seasons following the sun, the rain drawn from the ocean falling back through the rivers and streams. Within us too, the daily rhythms and flow of our blood through artery and vein. Moving, flowing, living and dying in each cell, in each particle, each atom.

As we touch one part of the system, of the whole, so that touch impacts on the rest; the swirling mass of energy within energy. We may create, we may destroy but there is no holding back the stream of life sweeping forward. We may block it for a while, we may imprison, restrict or suppress but life is boundless, infinite and will endure.

Sport ... a Crucible of Learning

One of my very good friends and fellow member of my cricket club is the club 'quiz master'. When we go on tour or have any kind of event, there will always be a question or two that we are challenged with. This one came on the WhatsApp group and set me thinking: 'What has sport taught you most about life'? I posted the following on the group chat (and one of them was presented back to me at an Awards Night in a frame). So, I hope they resonate with you too.

Okay, here's an off the cuff starter. If you create the right culture and those involved – players, coaches, teachers, parents and spectators – are educated in that culture, you can play with and against anyone with honour and respect however intense or important the game. You can play to win AND play in the right way. If the culture is not built on that sense of a moral code, of honour and respect, then sport becomes a forum for our unfettered animal instincts. And so it is in life - we can choose to live in accordance with a moral code built on honour and respect or our animal instinct.

Next lesson. I have learnt from sport that it is easy to play any game from the sideline, from in front of the television. How easy it is to make the right choices, to be the expert when we watch from a distance in time or space. Sport has taught me to place different values on opinions and judgements based on distant observation or newspaper reports and the wisdom that comes from being a part of an experience. Sport, like life, is a crucible in which the metal is tested and shaped in the fires. And the more a sword is 'worked', the stronger it becomes. Sport can build courage and resilience not just for the game but for life. It can teach us how to live with 'triumph and disaster', the twin imposters and develop a maturity which cannot be found in any book or on any screen.

... and Friendship

Sport has always played a big part in my life. It has brought me immense enjoyment, and helped keep me physically, fit. Perhaps, most important of all, it has taught me so many lessons about leadership and about life. Lessons about emotional control, mental resilience, honour and respect.

It has also been the source, foundation and the rich colouring of many friendships. I wrote this for a dear friend's 40th birthday and it is based on a shared love of the great game of cricket. It does require a little knowledge of the game to make complete sense but hopefully, the meaning – a metaphor for life itself - will be clear enough. I like the idea of dedicating this poem to all those I have played with over the years.

Forty Overs Gone

So, the hard bounce and gloss have faded away
And the leather looks rough and worn.
For the knocks from the game have left their mark
With 40 overs gone.

The pace and swing at the start of play,
Fade as the overs go by
And the long hops you bowl as you find your line
Are smashed away hard and high.

It's a tough old game and the lessons are hard
'Till you learn the pattern of play
And you find that there's more than just strength and power
And bowling as fast as you may.

There's some who find that the wickets fall quick.
While, for others it all seems unfair,
But most of us find as the game unfolds
That we all have something to share.

And now is the time when the work starts to pay
As the leather, though soft, starts to shine
And the knowledge that's gained at the start of the day
Can be used to perfect length and line.

With 40 gone there's still 40 to go
And more if the game suits your style
So, look back and enjoy the toils of your work
And pause to reflect for a while.

Who knows what's in store for the rest of the match?
That's the magic we love in this game.
Some terrible muddle or glorious catch,
The picture is never the same.

It's a tough old game but it offers so much
So, get from each ball all you can.
There's another one waiting when this one is done
But you must use each as best as you can.

For what we forget in the heat of the game,
As we struggle for riches or fame,
Is that it's not the winning or losing that counts
But the way we take part in the game.

It's not just the runs but the friends that we make
On this beautiful turf where we play
That tell us the way that the game has gone
And the score at the end of the day.

So, there's a few overs gone since the first time we met
And we've had a good time there's no doubt.
But you know that there's something much deeper, my
friend,
And that's what these words are about

It's just a way of saying thank you
For all that you've brought to our game
For the laughter, the friendship and just being you,
Here's to forty more of the same.

God Bless.

... and So Much More

The focus of my charity work with Small Acts of Kindness is on providing leadership and life skills training for young people in Sri Lanka, Nepal, Rwanda and young refugees in Greece. The vehicle for the learning is sport. There are many reasons, but one is the way that it helps break down barriers of race, class and social background.

The Endless Fight

I love to be with my own team,
It feels so good inside.
They are my family, strong and true
And fill my heart with pride.

We are the heroes of this tale,
We stand for what is right.
And if we're challenged or provoked,
Then, we will stand and fight.

I see the others look at us,
Their eyes are filled with hate.
Their jealous words are just a mask,
They know we're truly great.

I know what goes in their mind,
I know they seek our gold.
But they're not worthy of our place,
They're from a different mould.

I hear their call and cries of pain,
Their feeble pleas for more.
But I will show no weakness
As I crush them to the floor.

Yet, now there's something changing,
Deep within my heart.
I start to feel at one with them
Not different and apart.

It began in such a simple way,
One afternoon of sport.
As one of them had joined my team
And side by side we fought.

We won our game and shared a drink,
We talked of family.
And suddenly my feelings changed,
This was a man like me.

I travelled to a jungle,
Far across the sea
And spoke with many people there,
To hear their history.

I learnt that all my stories,
Of dragons and mistrust,
Were built on fear and ignorance.
Worth nothing more than dust.

I met a girl in Kathmandu,
Who had suffered so much wrong.
Yet still she fought and worked,
That others might be strong.

I have learnt to look beyond
The colour of the skin.
To look beyond the differences
And see what lies within.

I have learnt to look beyond
The gender or the clothes.
To see the beauty in each heart,
A precious, golden rose.

The lesson that I share with you
And hope you take to heart,
Is to leave behind the stories
That hold us all apart

Take time to hear their real lives
And see what lies inside.
Look beyond the masks we wear,
The fear and greed we hide

You'll find the golden secret,
That one day all will see.
That we are not apart at all
But seeds from one great tree.

Then the stories for our children,
Will shed a different light.
They will bring us all together
And end the endless fight.

And Finally

I have not spoken about family and I'd like to finish with some words that I have written to express some of my feelings those closest to me.

I chose this first piece because, although it is very personal, I am sure that the sentiments are shared by many. My mother read these words on Mother's Day in 2011. She died a few months later. I would feel desperately sad if I had left them unsaid and I urge you to take the next opportunity to express your love for those who matter to you.

To Mum

Finding a card with the right words is just not possible. Nobody could find the words that I need; I am not sure they exist.

Another Mother's Day! Yet, today, there is a realization that there will not be many more. It is not something that we like to talk about but it is something we all have to face.

So, this is an opportunity to say what you mean and will always mean to me. Because, although we grow old and the world around us changes, there are some things that endure beyond all of this.

Your hair may have changed from auburn to grey and now to white, but you know that it is not your appearance that matters to me. Even the warm smile that touches my heart; you are so much more than this.

Your memory may be fading and the memories with them, but you know that it is not your intellect or mind that matter to me. Even the quiet loving word that warms me; you are so much more than this.

Your strength may be slowly ebbing, and you can no longer work or care as you once did, but you know that it is not your work or even your physical life that matters to me. You are so much more than this.

You are the one who gave me life. You are the eternal presence in my heart. In this life we are close but in the greater unfolding of the universe, our souls are forever joined. You have given me more than you will ever know and I love you more than I can possibly express. So, these few words will have to suffice.

Happy Mother's Day, today and always, from your son.

And, finally, in 2019, I became a grandfather and wrote some words as a gift to my beautiful little granddaughter. Again, the message was a very personal one but, as I re-read the words, I feel that they capture so much of what I would like to impart through my teaching work. So, with one or two small alterations, I want to share them with you.

Mingled in with my own words are exerts from two wonderful pieces'. 'My Law' which is 'attributed to a Maori and a poem by Paramahamsa Satyananda Saraswati about what it means to be a Sannyasin. I have called this.

My Blessing

What can I possibly say to you that might be of some use and guidance – your path will be so different to my own?

So, what I will say comes from the heart, for I can boast no great intellect or psychic talents. These words come from my own living experience, from a sense of a deep knowing about life, about who we are and why we are here.

In your heart and soul, you hold a precious seed of light, it is the essence of life itself. The world and people will swirl around you like shadows across the sun, but this part of you is timeless, indestructible; it holds the lessons from the past and all that you have become. It is your true nature.

You were. You will be! Know this while you are:
Your spirit has travelled both long and afar.
It came from the Source, to the Source it returns –
The Spark, which was lighted eternally burns.

It slept in a jewel. It leapt in a wave.
It roamed in the forest. It rose from the grave.
It took on strange garbs for long eons of years
And now in the soul of your self it appears.

Even in the dark moments, and there will be such times, hold to this centre; learn to listen to the quiet voice of your soul. It links you to those souls around you who will love and watch over you – and we will be there too. It links you to your eternal self and to the great Source from which you were born.

You are an invisible child of a thousand faces of love that floats over the swirling sea of life, surrounded by the meadows of winged shepherds, where divine love and beauty, the stillness of midnight summer's warmth pervades.

Life will bring you many experiences and, from all of them – the good and the not so good - you can learn; that is why we are here, to develop the soul. But be sure, you will face nothing that you are not strong enough to deal with. Always you will have the choice of how to face these experiences be they joyful or harsh and we can only urge you not to turn from them. Stay true to your own values and what you know in your heart to be 'the right thing'. Live life to the full, treat each breath each moment as a gift from the Gods; it is.

I shall be a witness, but never shall I run or turn from life, from me. Never shall I forsake myself or the timeless lessons that I have learnt. Nor shall I let the value of divine inspiration and being be lost. My rainbow covered bubble will carry me further than beyond the horizons, forever to serve, to love and to live.

There are some simple questions to ask yourself as you walk this path; they will help guide your steps. What experiences do you wish to have? How do you wish to grow – in mind, body and spirit? What will you contribute to the world around you – what talents do you have and how can you best use them to serve? Through these questions you will come to find your soul purpose and, when you do, strive with all your might to achieve it. Don't wait for the world to bring these gifts to you,

Shall I fall on bended knee and wait for someone to bless me with happiness and a life of golden dreams? No, I shall run into the desert of life with my arms open, sometimes falling, sometimes stumbling, but always picking myself up, a thousand times if necessary, sometimes happy, often life will burn me, often life will caress me tenderly and many of my days will be haunted with complications and obstacles and there will be moments so beautiful that my soul will weep in ecstasy.

The world is full of beauty and grace. The world is full of brutality and darkness. Be aware of your own humanity; never forget that we are divine beings living within the physical body of an animal, with animal instincts and drives. We all hold the seed of light and love and we all hold the seed of violence and darkness. Feed and nurture the one that you wish to live within you. Our world is what we have chosen to make it and our future is what we choose it to be. As long as you listen to your heart, live with love, seek to serve then you can know that your soul will sing with joy and the angels will sing with you.

Walk freely but with a care. There are many wonderful, sacred scripts that can help guide us. Read them, meditate on them but do not be bound by any one belief. There are many 'false prophets' and tricksters who will seek to win your trust, be careful of them. Test everything that you read, see or hear against your own logic, your own inner guide.

You are your own Devil, you are your own God
You fashioned the paths your footsteps have trod.
And no one can save you from Error or Sin
Until you have hark'd to the Spirit within.

May your life be a long, full and happy one. May you discover and fully express the talents that you have and may you know the joy of using them in the service of others. May you love passionately and deeply, and may you always know that you are loved and watched over, in this life and the next.

With my love and blessing,

Peter

The Next Stage of the Journey

I hope that you have enjoyed my attempt to capture some moments in my life. To explore more of your own spiritual impulse or find your own path to peace and harmony you might be interested in my work as a healer at

Chalybeate Healing

www.chalybeatehealing.com

To explore how you might contribute to the quest to bring more light and love into the world, you might be interested in my charity work at

Small Acts of Kindness

www.saok.org.uk

I hope that our paths may cross, and we may walk together on the mountain.